I0472930

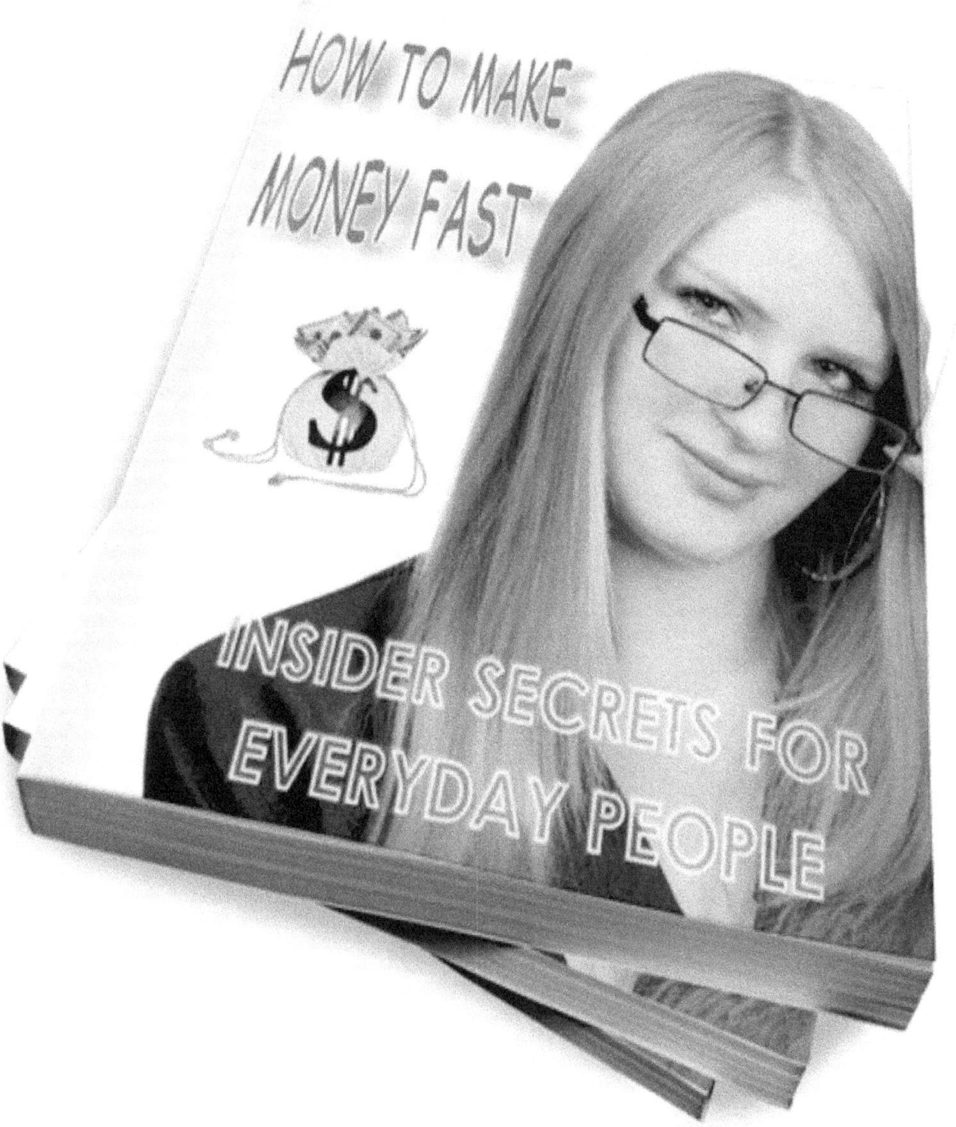

HOW TO MAKE MONEY FAST

INSIDER SECRETS FOR EVERYDAY PEOPLE

HOW TO MAKE MONEY FAST

INSIDER SECRETS FOR EVERYDAY PEOPLE

By

C W Masterpiece

TABLE OF CONTENTS

By

C W Masterpiece

2. MONEY ILLUSTRATION B

B. STATE-OF-THE-ART INFORMATION

C. QUICK MONEY MAKING

    1. UNLIMITED INCOME POTENTIAL

    2. LIMITED OVERHEAD

    3. NO INVENTORY

    4. LIMITED RISK

III. GLOBAL MARKETPLACE

A. MONEY ILLUSTRATION C

B. MONEY ILLUSTRATION D

By

C W Masterpiece

IV. TRAFFIC

A. MORE CLICKS VIA FORUMS

B. MORE CLICKS VIA BLOGS

C. MORE CLICKS VIA ARTICLES

D. MORE CLICKS VIA VIDEOS

V. SEARCH ENGINE OPTIMIZATION (SEO) TECHNIQUES

A. YOUR ARTICLES USED BY OTHERS

B. SUBMIT TO ALL SEARCH ENGINES

CONCLUSION

By

C W Masterpiece

HOW TO MAKE MONEY FAST -

INSIDER SECRETS FOR EVERYDAY PEOPLE

INTRODUCTION

How to make money fast is a question many people are

asking. For example, making $100 a day is a dream for

a great majority of people nowadays. More and more

people worldwide want to make money fast in independent

ways.

By

C W Masterpiece

This idea of independent money making and flexible work

hours is quite attractive. There is more quality time to enjoy

life, more time to spend with family and friends, more

time for traveling, and more time to pursue one's favorite

pastimes.

Indeed, working from home offers many benefits, freedom

to allocate your time and the opportunity to make as much

money was you want, without limits.

Yes, there is a lifestyle change from the traditional work

world. Imagine. You may wake up whenever you want,

have your coffee, tea, or breakfast smoothie, have your run,

By

C W Masterpiece

walk or go to the gym, turn on your computer, work designated

hours online, and then spend your time with your family,

friends and hobbies.

Too good to be true? Not really. Too many people wrongfully

think that making good money online is unattainable. They

think that there are too many requirements that they do not

have such as special knowledge, a website and huge

investments.

The fact is --- you can start making hundreds and thousands of

dollars per month with no upfront fees and even without a

website.

By

C W Masterpiece

With this knowledge, if given the chance, the majority

worldwide wouldn't think twice about grabbing such an

opportunity.

Why not ask yourself:

1. Do I have a spare space room or a kitchen table

   in my home?

2. Do I have a telephone line?

3. Do I have a computer with an internet connection?

If you have these three things, you have the essentials of an

By

C W Masterpiece

office from which you can start making money fast starting

right now.

In this book, you discover insider secrets of how to make

money fast each and every day by fully utilizing the potentials

of Affiliate Relationships, Affiliate Marketing and the Internet.

I. AFFILIATE RELATIONSHIPS

Have you ever heard of Affiliate Programs?

An Affiliate Program is a business advertising relationship

By

C W Masterpiece

between a company or business and the Affiliate (You). The

company is the advertiser and the Affiliate brings in the

customers by driving traffic. The company rewards the Affiliate

for driving traffic or customers to the company and their

products and services.

In other words, the advertiser pays the Affiliate

and the Affiliate sends traffic to the advertiser in return.

Simply put, it's about paying commissions to people who help

the business to make sales. That's it.

Once you have everything all set up and ready to go, you can

begin making an income from your efforts. In Affiliate

By

C W Masterpiece

Marketing, the company pays the Affiliate a commission or a

percentage of the sale. For example, a beverage company may

pay you 10% of all sales that you, as an Affiliate, generate for

them.

This is how it works. When a business decides that they would

like to have some help selling their product or service, they will

then start an Affiliate program. When they do this, they are

allowing others to sign up and sell their products or a

particular service that they are offering.

However, the company that needs the help selling the product,

By

C W Masterpiece

will then give all of their Affiliates a unique ID number that they

can use in their links, and so that the company can see who the

sale came from when a sale is made from an Affiliate.

With this unique ID number, the Affiliate can then use multiple

ways to market products and services. It is not difficult to

choose affiliate marketing programs with which you want

to associate and start making money. It good to choose

something that you know about, have passion for and about

which you can become known as an expert.

The more passionate you are about the service or product, the

better. Passion is powerful.

By

C W Masterpiece

Many companies in the United States and abroad have Affiliate

Marketing programs. As an Affiliate, you can generate traffic to

your websites, the company's websites, increase sales and/or

views and you make money. These programs offer ways for

Affiliates to make money through links, forums, articles, blogs,

videos, among others. These are usually free and worth using.

Remember, the more you make, the more they make. Affiliate

relationships like these should be a WIN-WIN for all parties.

This relationship is commonly referred to as Affiliate

Marketing.

Affiliate Marketing is one of the most cost effective ways to

start your money making empire today.

By

C W Masterpiece

14

I. AFFILIATE MARKETING STARTS THE MONEY FLOW

One of the first things to do to start your money making as an

Affiliate is to become an Affiliate with your choice of companies

such as:

Amazon	Clickbank	OfferVault	Commission Junction
Walmart	PetMart	GEICO	Macy's
Panasonic	Chase	Netflix	Clinique

By

C W Masterpiece

JC Penney	1800PetMeds	AT & T	Capital One
CITI	Magic Jack	Equifax	The Limited
HSN	Budget	Foot Locker	Western Union
Omaha Steaks	Payless	Hotwire	Crocs.com
Bank of America	iTunes	Snuggle	Barnes & Nobles
Expedia	Golfsmith	Credit.com	Florsheim
Discover	TheHomeDepot	Dish Network	Perry Ellis
Hotels.com	ShopAdidas.com	Game Stop	Elizabeth Arden
Best Buy	DirecTV	H&R Block	Sirius Radio
Gamefly	ScotTrade	TheNorthFace	Mikasa

Let's see a simple example of how this works when an Affiliate

drives the following visitors to the company's website in one

By

C W Masterpiece

day:

VISITORS	# OF SALES	$ PER SALE	TOTAL
200	10	$10	$100

So, in this example, the Affiliate has made $100 dollars in one

day.

At a minimum, let's say the Affiliate repeats the same thing for

5 days.

That's $100 x 5 days = $500 for the week. Not bad.

By

C W Masterpiece

When armed with state-of-the-art information and a few

technical how-to's, you, too, can use Affiliate Marketing to start

making money fast.

QUICK MONEY MAKING WITH AFFILIATE MARKETING

Affiliates are excited about the quick money making

opportunities offered by Affiliate Marketing.

1. Unlimited Income Potential

By

C W Masterpiece

Unlike a paid job, where one's monthly income is limited and is

mainly determined by whether one goes to work or not. With

Affiliate Marketing, an Affiliate leads traffic to a company's

website without having to lift a finger after providing the

appropriate ad copy and link. An affiliate's earning potential

is, indeed, limitless.

2. Limited Overhead

Unlike other money making ventures, one can start Affiliate

Marketing on a shoe string. As an affiliate, you can make money

based on your hard work. You are the one rewarded for your

By

C W Masterpiece

efforts, not a boss or a group of shareholders. You don't have to

worry about financial risk. The company with which you

affiliate will take care of all the details, allowing you to

promote, drive traffic, sell and make money.

With limited overhead, you can use Affiliate Marketing to

increase your bank balance, not someone else's. Affiliate

Marketing is just the way to go for fast easy cash flow.

3. No Need For Inventory

There is no need for the Affiliate to have to worry about

By

C W Masterpiece

inventory, product maintenance or product management. The

advertiser business does it all.

4. Limited Risk

Perhaps one of the attractive things for an Affiliate is the

limited risk. Affiliate marketing provide several advantages in

this area.

You are marketing products that are already in existence.

Known brands are not so hard to promote or sell especially

if they have a good reputation. Trusted products will attract

By

C W Masterpiece

customers much faster than something new and unknown.

Affiliate marketing takes the risk away.

You're usually given all you need in the form of leaflets,

catalogs, ads, banners and other product information. You are

also likely given good advice on how best to sell the products.

With affiliate marketing, there should be a representative on

hand that you can contact for support and advice. This allows

you time to concentrate on what needs to be done ---

making profits and creating continual cash flow.

You are paid according to how well you perform. You do not

need to worry how the business is performing overall. You

By

C W Masterpiece

make your money based on your visitors and/or

customers. The companies with which you affiliate are usually

well-established so you don't have to worry about them closing

down on you without notice.

III. GLOBAL MARKETPLACE

As an Affiliate, you have access to companies and customers

worldwide. Can you see the unlimited income possibilities?

You can set up your Affiliate Marketing to work every single

second of the day while targeting a worldwide market! What

By

C W Masterpiece

could be better than that?

ILLUSTRATION OF THE GLOBAL MONEY ADVANTAGE FOR THE AFFILIATE

Let's take our beginning example where the Affiliate drove

traffic to only one company in one country. Look at the results

when the Affiliate drives traffic to one company in two

countries:

COUNTRY	VISITORS	# OF SALES	$ PER SALE	SUB-TOTAL
1	200	10	$10	$100
2	200	10	$10	$100
			TOTAL	$200

By

C W Masterpiece

In this example, the Affiliate has made $200 dollars in one day simply by adding another company. Ofcourse, the company may be in a different country or in the same country. It really does not matter.

The Affiliate repeats the same thing for 5 days.

That's $200 x 5 days = $1000 for the week.

This is recurring monthly income. Once again, not bad!

IV. TRAFFIC

HOW TO GET CUSTOMERS TO YOUR WEBSITE AND/OR THE COMPANY'S WEBSITE?

By

C W Masterpiece

One of the smartest ways to get customers to visit a company's

website is to place your Affiliate link on your own website.

Where you place your Affiliate links on your website can really

make a difference on how many clicks you end up getting and,

since every click means money for you, this is an important

aspect of your Affiliate Marketing plan.

According to the research, the most effective Affiliate links or

your own website links are text links. That's right, plain text

links. Simply, write a helpful forum comment, a powerful blog

post, write a great article or make a short video about the

By

C W Masterpiece

product or something related to the product and insert your

Affiliate link. Interested readers and viewers then see your

link as they are reading or viewing and they click on it.

Ways to get more clicks include:

   * Compile a list of product-related forums

   * Become a regular participant in those forums

   * Comment when appropriate, including your Affiliate link

   * Compile a list of product-related blogs

   * Comment when appropriate, including your Affiliate link

   * Write an article about the product, including your Affiliate   link

   * Assure that your article and your affiliate link work   effectively   together

   * Compile a list of Article Directories

By

C W Masterpiece

27

* Submit your article in those directories

* Make a video about the product, including your Affiliate

  link --- using your same article content.

*Submit your video to YouTube, similar channels and video directories.

* Get your website high on search engine.

* Convince visitors to click on all your links.

GET MORE CLICKS VIA FORUMS

If you are ready to put in some time and effort, you are ready to

learn how to transform your life and start making money as an

Affiliate Marketer online.

One of the easiest ways to begin to generate Affiliate

By

C W Masterpiece

commissions is to post comments in forums related to the

product(s) that you have chosen to market. Observe how

others in the forums are participating in the conversation and

how other marketers are using their links in their signatures.

Follow the routine.

At all times, you should browse the topics where you can

provide useful tips and answers to the questions that people

ask. If you have used the product that you want to promote

and you are happy with it, you should tell others about its

benefits and how it helped you.

It's not enough to post a couple of comments with expectations

By

C W Masterpiece

of earning thousands of dollars in commissions. Plan on

selecting several forums that interest you and keep visiting

them and posting comments for at least a month.

Avoid trying to sell your product ---but help people.

When you have posted hundreds of comments, people will treat

you as an expert and the sales will start to come in.

GET FAST CLICKS VIA BLOGS

After you have spent some time posting comments to forums,

you will notice that some topics and questions are asked again

and again.

By

C W Masterpiece

Since you already know how to help people, you should start writing posts on blogs on the list you compiled and promote your affiliate links.

Yes, join the crowd and blog about your website, product, service or subject. Blogging is an internet advertising method that is popular. All you have to do is sign up for "no cost" blogging accounts, post and you are all set. Ofcourse, the more blog posts you write, the more clicks you get, the more sales you send to the companies, the more money you make.

By

C W Masterpiece

GET FAST CLICKS VIA ARTICLES

Together with your active participation in forums and blogs,

start writing articles and promote your affiliate links in them.

The way this works is you write an article, insert your affiliate

link and/or website link, submit your article to e-zines and get

traffic from visitors.

It's as simple as that. Continue to repeat, repeat and repeat

again. The more e-zines you post your link in, the more visitors,

the more clicks and the more money.

By

C W Masterpiece

Writing and posting articles is that ONE method most Affiliates

start with in order to achieve clicks to drive traffic for more

customers, more sales and terrific pay checks.

There is nothing more effective.

When writing the perfect article for Affiliate Marketing

purposes, use the following as a general guide:

  *Research your keywords

  *Compile your main list of keywords

  *Write articles which are keyword rich

  *Write attention grabbing headlines (most important part of   your article)

  *Write great articles quickly

  *Write articles 300-350 words in length.

By

C W Masterpiece

*Write great articles quickly

*Maintain the reader's interest throughout

GET FAST CLICKS VIA VIDEOS

Now, use what you have commented about in forums, what you

have posted on blogs and what you have written about in

articles and make videos on the same subjects. Follow the same

procedure of including your Affiliate link so that viewers of

your videos will click, purchase and become loyal customers.

Fast money comes rolling in.

V. SEARCH ENGINE OPTIMIZATION (SEO) TECHNIQUES

By

C W Masterpiece

34

If you want become a super Affiliate bringing in good money automatically month after month, it helps to use as much search engine optimization (SEO) as you can.

To use search engine optimization techniques when writing and publishing your articles assures higher rankings. The higher your rankings, the more viewers see your Affiliate links, thus, the more clicks, the more sales and the more fast money making.

When hiring a writer to write articles for you, you may choose one who already knows about SEO or you can supply them with a list of keywords and let them know where they

By

C W Masterpiece

should be placed and how many times they should be

repeated throughout the article.

Writing your articles for search engines will help them rank

higher when someone searches for a keyword relating to your

subject, which means that you will receive more visitors

because more people will actually see your Affiliate link.

It is a fact that most visitors don't look past page one of the

search engines and by the third page, there is practically no

audience left for you to promote to.

What this means for those on pages three and higher is no

traffic. This is why it is very important for you as an Affiliate to

make sure that your articles are prepared in a way that will

By

C W Masterpiece

eventually get them to page one of the search engines.

GET FAST CLICKS BY LETTING OTHERS USE YOUR ARTICLES

Allow others to use your articles, along with your byline

which tells visitors who wrote it and how they can contact you.

This helps to promote your own website, your Affiliate link and

bring you in traffic through the search engine optimization and

promotional efforts of others. This means absolutely free

marketing for you just for writing a quick article about a

subject with which you are already familiar.

The more people using your article as content on their website,

the more potential traffic you will receive. These webmasters

By

C W Masterpiece

will probably be using SEO techniques, banner exchanges, and

possibly even a Pay-Per-Click campaign to get visitors to their

websites. And you get to benefit from their marketing efforts.

These are advertising methods that neither take a lot of time or

a lot of money and they will be absolutely free for you just

because you placed your articles where others could use them.

Text linking is not just cheap. It is virtually free! Why not let

someone text link your site and return the favor. Remember,

we are talking about added revenue here. Never

underestimate the power of link exchange. This is a low

cost traffic source that people tend to overlook. As a smart

By

C W Masterpiece

Affiliate, take advantage of link exchanges.

An easy way to get more link exchanges is to type your

website's keywords in a major search engine, visit each and

every search engine and ask for the link exchanges.

The internet has many places where you may post your article

so that others may view and/or use it. Place your articles on

every single one of these sites so that you can reach as many

webmasters as possible.

GET FAST CLICKS BY SUBMITTING TO ALL SEARCH ENGINES

By

C W Masterpiece

Submission to all search engines is cheap and dependable. If

you submit your website link to all search engines ---

not just Google, Yahoo, Bing, your audience reach expands

quickly.   Include the small search engines.

This provides you greater chances to get bigger results. You

must keep in mind that the search engine giants can easily

overlook your site, so this internet advertising method might

just be the right one for you.

CONCLUSION

You may choose any of the above methods to start

your independent means of making money fast. Whether

By

C W Masterpiece

you choose to establish Affiliate relationships, together

with Affiliate Marketing, the Internet and/or any combination

of these methods, success is there for you to start making

money fast today and continuing for years to come.

By

C W Masterpiece

www.ingramcontent.com/pod-product-compliance
Lightning Source LLC
Chambersburg PA
CBHW071549170526
45166CB00004B/1605